How to Identify
A New Testament
Local Church

How to Identify
A New Testament
Local Church

Kenneth G. Symes

ARPress
ILLUMINATING IDEAS
EMPOWERING VOICES

ARPress
45 Dan Road Suite 5
Canton MA 02021

Hotline: 1(888) 821-0229
Fax: 1(508) 545-7580

Ordering Information:

Quantity sales. Special discounts are available on quantity purchases by corporations, associations, and others. For details, contact the publisher at the address above.

Printed in the United States of America.

ISBN-13:   Paperback   979-8-89330-661-3
                eBook   979-8-89330-660-6

Library of Congress Control Number: 2024902488

All Bible quotations are taken from The King James Version

Table of Contents

e
PREFACE

I never planned to write a book. Now I have written several only because I have been prompted by the Holy Spirit to do so. Each of the books I have written were written out of a concern I have had regarding issues in the church of my day. That is certainly true of this book. I have had enough formal education in the Christian realm to have earned a Doctorate degree which I do not have because I never really wanted one. In all of that formal education I cannot recall ever being given a clear Biblical definition of a Biblical New Testament Local Church. In recent years I have met and talked with several people whom I believe to be born again believers who have been turned off by the institutional church of our day. Even as I have traveled (and continue to do so) only in "fundamental" circles I have been dismayed by some biblical contradictions between doctrine and practice in many churches.

This led me to search for a Biblical definition of what is a New Testament local church. The burning question on my heart was: "How can anyone plant and build such a church if they do not know what one is supposed to be?" This led me to write this book. I am aware that there is much more that can be written on this subject. However, I believe I have laid out the basic principles that give us a clear and understandable definition of what a New Testament local church should be. I trust that this will be helpful to you as you consider your local church, or as you are searching for one in which to worship and serve that truly stands on the teachings of God's Word.

Special thanks to Dr. & Mrs. Nat Thompson for the help they have given me to be sure this dissertation is well written both in content and in the writing form. Thanks to my wife who still puts up with me as I write. Several years ago she told me that she would divorce me if I wrote another book. Since then I have written at least three more books. This year we will celebrate our 64th Wedding anniversary.

May this book be a blessing to all who read and study it.

e
HOW TO IDENTIFY A NEW TESTAMENT LOCAL CHURCH?

Kenneth G. Symes

INTRODUCTION

Recently I was speaking with a man probably in his early sixties. I know him to be a born again believer. I have known him for many years. Until just a few years ago, he was active in what I believed to be a fundamental church. It concerned me that he was no longer involved in a local church. As we talked, I learned that he was still actively witnessing and sharing the gospel. I sensed that he was making a valid effort to stay in fellowship with the Lord.

We talked about why he was no longer involved with a local church. He said: "I find most local churches are no longer functioning as what I believe to be a true New Testament local church." As we talked further, I determined that his understanding of what a New Testament Church was supposed to be was right on target as far as he went with it. He went on and shared with me that what he sees in most local churches today is that they have lost their biblical vision of what a local church should be. With this I could not disagree.

He admitted that there probably are still a few local fellowships out there that are standing on and practicing what the Bible teaches regarding what a New Testament local church should be. But he was so turned off that he had lost any desire to try to locate a local church where he could comfortably be a part. I pointed out to him that it is God's plan for believers to be an active part of a sound local church sharing with him Hebrews 10:19-25. His response was that anywhere that two or three believers gather together constitutes a church.

Though there is some truth in that, the New Testament church, as we find it in the book of Acts and Ephesians, was much more. Clearly it is an organized fellowship of believers led, essentially, by a pastor.

In Acts 6:1-7 we see organization. There are those whose primary responsibility is the preaching and teaching of the word and others who assumed other responsibilities (vv.1-4). When Barnabas found Saul, he took him to Antioch. *"And it came to pass, that a whole year they assembled themselves with the church, and taught much people."* (Acts 11:26). This demonstrates an organized fellowship where the believers regularly met, not only for worship but for service. Note also Acts 14:23; 15:4; 16:5; 20:28.

There are many folks who believe themselves to be Christians, and they may be, who use the Hebrews 10 passage as an excuse to not become involved in an organized church. Their problem is that they only see half of what the church is called out to be. They see it only as a place of worship. In this sense it is true that two or three could gather together to worship the Lord. But most of those using this excuse for not participating in a Biblical local church are not even doing that. A true Biblical local church gathers for worship, but they also join together to serve the Lord. According to Hebrews 10:23-25 they gather to strengthen their faith (vs. 23). Further, they meet to encourage one another to love and be involved in doing good works (vs 24).

To exhort is to admonish and/or advise. In the positive sense each member is called to encourage other members as they walk in the faith. In John 14:23 Jesus is recorded as saying: *"If a man love me, he will keep my words"* and in this a believer is blest: *"and my father will love him, and we will come unto him, and make our abode with him."* Here is what Jesus teaches in this verse: <u>My love for Jesus is seen in direct proportion to my willingness to obediently serve Him.</u> That takes an organized local fellowship. We will deal further with this thought later in this study.

In John 15:12 Jesus said: *"This is my commandment, that ye love one another, as I have loved you."* The word translated "love" is "agape" which is God's love and is unconditional. With this spirit we are called to "exhort" one another and this takes an organized church.

When we moved to St. Petersburg, FL back in the mid-eighties to begin a new work, we found a lot of folks, several of whom were Jewish, who had become believers but who were not involved in a local church. In most instances, I suspected that whoever led them to the

Lord did not seek to disciple them and to get them involved in a sound local fellowship. These new believers were not growing in the Lord. They were still just immature babes in Christ. Several were involved in a Messianic Synagogue where the emphasis was on maintaining their Jewish distinctions so they were not getting good sound biblical teaching. They all began to regularly attend our Hebrew/ Christian Bible study which we were holding, at that time, in our home. They were amazed at the teaching of God's word. Those attending the Messianic Synagogue said to us that they had never heard any of what we were teaching them. The rest were just amazed at the truths they were learning from the Bible. After getting them stabilized in God's word we began to plant them in what we believed were sound local churches. This clearly shows the importance to become involved in a good, sound Bible believing local church so that new believers can grow in the Lord.

Two or three believers, in one sense do constitute a church. But this is not the church described in the book of Acts as a local church. We shall more fully look at why this is a true statement later as we consider the purpose and ministry of a true New Testament local church.

The intended purpose of this book is to help the reader understand what the Bible clearly teaches about a believer's involvement in a local church and what the Bible teaches about what a New Testament local church is. This gives the reader foundational information so that he/she will be able to determine whether or not a particular church is truly a "New Testament" local church, worthy of his/her participation and support.

At the very outset of this treatise, it must be stated that there is no perfect local church because they are made up of imperfect people. Every local church has its issues. Our purpose is not to criticize, but to establish what constitutes a biblically maturing New Testament local church. We desire to present a very clear goal for every local church to seek to attain. We also want to give believers the information to determine if a particular local church adheres at least to the fundamentals as clearly laid out in God's word. It is an interesting fact that with all of the formal biblical education I have received over the years, I was never specifically taught what a biblical New Testament local church should be. I wonder how many pastors today have a sufficient depth of understanding of what the Bible teaches on this subject. This deficit helps create the problem that the local church faces today. After all, how can we know how to build that which we do not really understand?

We must also understand at the outset of this treatise that God's purpose in creating man was for fellowship as this is a fundamental Bible truth (Gen. 2:8, 9). Psalm 16:11 speaks of why that relationship should be important to us. *"Thou wilt show me the path of life: In thy presence is fullness of joy; and at thy right hand there are pleasures for evermore."* In John 14:23 Jesus said: *"If a man love me, he will keep my words: and my Father will love him, and we will come into him, and make our abode with him."* Please note that the Greek word translated "love" is "agapao" depicting God's love which is unconditional. So what Jesus is saying here is that if we will love Him unconditionally the result will be personal fellowship with Him.

Remember, Christianity is not a religion, it is a relationship. Religion is man's effort to find and please God. It is ritual and rules, the goal of which is to earn one's way to eternal life, a humanly impossible task. Regarding religion, the Bible states: *"But we are all as an unclean thing, and all our righteousnesses* (good works) *are as filthy rags; and we all do fade as a leaf; and our iniquities, like the wind, have taken us away."* (Isaiah 64:6). In Isaiah 57:12 God stated: *I will declare thy righteousness, and thy works; for they shall not profit thee."* Paul stated it this way in Romans 6:23: *"The wages of sin is death; but the gift of God is eternal life through Jesus Christ our Lord."* Religion does not save! The true God created man for fellowship which results in fullness of joy and pleasures that go into eternity. And that fellowship is to be not only with God, but also with other believers. Should this not be the heart of the local church? Only God can overcome, on our behalf, the wages of sin. And only God can transform a new believer into the image of His dear son (II Corinthians 3:18). This is important for us to understand if we are going to understand why God created the local church and laid out His plan for its existence as He has done.

Let us now begin our study of what God states is a New Testament local Church.

e

CHAPTER 1

WHAT IS THE CHURCH?

The word "church" in Greek is *ekklesia*, a called out assembly. In the pre-Christian era *ekklesia* was used to describe a regular assembly of the whole body of citizens in a free city-state who were called out by a herald for the discussion and decision of public business. A good biblical example of this is found in Acts 19:32-41. This certainly indicates organization and leadership to be an integral part of a local church. In James 2:2, among other places, it is tied to the concept of the Jewish Synagogue, the formal religious gathering of Judaism and here it is translated *"assembly"* as is *ekklesia* in Acts 19:32-41 where it is used three times to depict a lawful gathering.. The comparable Hebrew term is *kahal* and is used of the congregation of Israel (cf. Lev. 16:15). To the Greek it suggested a self-governing, democratic society; to the Jew, a theocratic society whose members were subjects of the heavenly King. In either case, it is clear that the Bible teaches that the local church is an organized entity with leadership and a clear purpose. This is precisely the sense of the word *ekklesia*, the only word consistently used to identify the biblical NT local church.

It is generally used in the New Testament in its corporate sense. It is important, however, to note that nowhere in the New Testament is "church" used to denote a physical structure. It is always used to describe a group of believers who gather together for the purpose of carrying on the Lord's work, which is much more than just the act of worship. To quote Hebrews 10:23-25 and state it teaches that anywhere two or three gather together to worship is a local church is denying the real meaning of the passage. A true local church is more than a gathering to worship. It is clear that the local church met regularly in a specific place, implying a common physical location, to both worship **and** carry on the Lord's work. In the early years of the church they were "home churches." In a later chapter we will consider what the Bible says the local New Testament church is to be about beyond the acts of worship.

TWO ASPECTS OF THE LOCAL CHURCH

It is also important to understand the two aspects of the local church as taught in Scripture. There is the "spiritual" church which is constituted of all who have been truly born again, (the true believers,) holding sound doctrine whose lives have been transformed by the indwelling presence of the Holy Spirit. This is often described in the Bible as the "body of Christ." (Romans 12:2-4; I Corinthians 12:27; Ephesians 1:22-23; 4:12; Colossians 1:24.)

But, even here, we need to note there are two parts to the spiritual church. Paul speaks of this as recorded in I Corinthians 3:1 which reads: *"And I, brethren, could not speak unto you as unto spiritual, but as unto carnal, even as unto babes in Christ."* It is clear that he is speaking to those whom he considers believers as he calls them "brethren" recognizing some as carnal (immature, "babes") and others as spiritual or mature in the faith.

Note Paul's further statement: *"That we henceforth be no more children, tossed to and fro, and carried about with every doctrine, by the sleight of men, and cunning craftiness, whereby they lie in wait to deceive."* (Ephesians 4:14). The context of this passage is that Paul is speaking of *"the unity of the faith."*

One characteristic of a carnal Christian is their lack of understanding of the doctrines of the faith. The verse under consideration is talking about young believers (children in the faith) who are not familiar with what is true doctrine. They are weak in the faith and are thus easily led astray. They often create false issues, division and dissension in the fellowship. Paul clarifies this further in I Corinthians 3:3ff. He states: *"For ye are yet carnal: for whereas there is among you envying, and strife, and divisions, are ye not yet carnal, and walk as men?"* Carnal Christians are the result of a clear lack of discipleship. Is there not a parallel between the new birth and the physical birth? Is it not true that God's plan for a new baby is to be taken home and there discipled into the

7

human family? Of this subject we will further explore at a later point in this treatise.

Then, there are those in the institutional local church who have never been saved (received the new birth). How often have we heard a Church leader make the statement that today there is a substantial percentage in almost every local church who are not saved. They are the tares growing with the wheat. In Matthew 13:24ff Jesus talks about this in relation to the Kingdom which, as we shall see later, has a direct relationship to the church. Jesus talks about the wheat and tares growing together lest pulling the tares would destroy the wheat. This often occurs when the soul winner gives the one who has made a profession of faith assurance that they are saved. Pastor Nat Thompson taught me years ago that I honestly cannot give assurance of salvation to anyone. Note that Ephesians 1:13 teaches that only the Holy Spirit can give a new believer assurance of salvation. *"In whom ye also trusted, after that ye heard the word of truth, the gospel of your salvation: in whom also after that ye believed, ye were sealed with the Holy Spirit of promise"* (Romans 8:23; II Corinthians 1:22; I John 3:18-24). When a soul winner attempts to give a potentially new believer assurance that he is saved he is usurping the authority of the Holy Spirit. In doing so, he is sinning and becoming a part of a greater problem down the road.

Hence it is true that in most local churches (if not in all) true believers, babes and mature believers, are growing together with many unbelievers. Thus, we now can understand why there is no perfect local church.

In a later chapter we will consider what the work of a local church is to be in dealing with this issue, as stated in the New Testament. Hopefully, this will help us to better understand how to deal with both the carnal and false believer within the framework and biblical purpose of the local church. In this process we will also note the priorities that the Bible clearly establishes regarding this work.

e

CHAPTER 2

THE FIRST USE OF THE TERM CHURCH

It is important that we consider the first New Testament reference to the church as this will help us to understand the three foundational principles of a New Testament local church. In other words, these basic principles must be operational in a local church if it is to be a biblical New Testament local church. These are the true foundational fundamentals upon which any New Testament local church must stand.

The first use of the term *"church"* is found in Matthew 16:18 which reads: *"And I say also unto thee, that thou art Peter, and upon this rock I will build my church."* It appears that what Jesus had in mind was a body associated with His words *"the kingdom"*. Though He was speaking to Jews in this passage He was not speaking of a synagogue as He stated: *"Upon this rock I will build my Church."* This is clearly a different kind of assembly as we may note by the three concepts which are taught here that can only be applied to the local church. In a study of these three concepts we will note that these three concepts mentioned are the three foundational pillars of a New Testament local church.

THE DECLARATION

The "ekklesia" (church) consists first of those confessing Jesus as the Christ, the Messiah, Deity. The "rock" of which Jesus speaks in verse 18 is the confession that Jesus is the Christ. In I Cor. 10:4, while speaking of the Jew's deliverance from Egypt (see verses 1-3) Paul stated: *"And did all drink the same spiritual drink: for they drank of the same spiritual Rock that followed them; and that Rock was Christ,"* thus indicating that the "Rock" is a type of Christ. It is essential that we understand that Messiah (Hebrew) and Christ (Greek) are one and the same (John 1:41; 4:25).

The Hebrew Scriptures (OT) openly teach that Messiah is God. He is spoken of as the Son of God in Proverbs 30:4 and Psalm 2:7. Messiah is described as the sinless Son of God in Isaiah 50:5-9 and Isaiah 53:11. He is clearly God in Micah 5:2 and Isaiah 9:6. But the clearest reference is found in Zechariah 12:10. *"And I will pour upon the son of David, and upon the inhabitants of Jerusalem, the spirit of grace and of supplications: and they shall look upon me whom they have pierced, and they shall mourn for him, as one mourneth for his only son."* Could Zechariah do that? Of course not! Verse 9 clearly shows that it could not be Zechariah. But who could it be? The "I" here can only be God because the antecedent of "me" is the preceding "I" who is clearly God. Thus to confess Jesus to be the Christ (Messiah) is to confess Him to be God!

John, in defining an overcomer, a born-again believer, wrote: *"Who is he that overcometh the world, but he that believeth that Jesus is the Son of God"* (I John 5:5). John clearly states that apart from the recognition of the deity of Jesus one cannot be saved. This is the foundational truth upon which the church is built and all spiritual blessings flow. A local church is not biblical except it holds firmly to this great truth. As it is a necessary truth for salvation, why is it seldom mentioned in any presentation of the Gospel? This truth denotes the spiritual element that must be a foundational part of every local church according to Jesus: (Matthew 16:16-18). Therefore, if a local church is not standing firmly on this truth it is not a biblical New Testament local church.

THE DESIGN

Second, Jesus stated that this new society (the church) was to be representative of the heavenly kingdom realized on earth. This is the essence of the first phrase of verse 19: *"And I will give unto thee the keys of the kingdom of heaven..."* The idea of the keys is that it takes a Peter-like faith in Jesus to be admitted into the kingdom of Heaven. As we have already seen in I John 5:5 no one can be saved apart from recognizing that Jesus is God. This denotes how one enters into the church, the "body of Christ".

But the local church is clearly stated to be more than just a belief. This new faith results in a transformed person living in fellowship with the Creator and other believers. Paul stated in I Corinthians 5:17 *"Therefore if any man be in Christ, he is a new creature, old things are passed away; behold, all things are become new"* (Romans 8:9; Ephesians 2:13- 22). Thus the local church, as a fellowship, is also to be an example to the world of the coming Kingdom of God which emphasizes the importance of an organized fellowship.

We may further note that Jesus speaks of the Kingdom 124 times just in the Gospels. There are 7 references to the Kingdom in Acts and another 18 references recorded in the Epistles, plus an additional five references in the Book of the Revelation. So, the word "kingdom" is found 154 times in the New Testament which certainly constitutes a major theme.

Consider the use of this term in the Gospels. In John 18: 36 Jesus speaks of the kingdom as not of this world. In Matthew it is called "the heavenly kingdom". Also in Matthew the use of the phrase "the gospel of the Kingdom" was speaking of Jesus offering to Israel the promised earthly kingdom which was prophetically necessary to be done at this time. Had Israel received Jesus as their Messiah/King, there would have been no necessity for the Church Age. That is why the church was never revealed in the Old Testament and why it is a New Testament mystery revealed through Paul.

This was God's purpose. The Jews were to evangelize the world but they did not. Jonah is a great example of their attitude toward Gentiles. Thus it was necessary in God's plan, to reach the world with His redeeming love, to set Israel aside nationally, so that the Gentiles could be offered God's redemptive love (Romans 11:11).

In Mark 11:10 the author defines the Lord's use of the term "the kingdom of God" as offering the Kingdom to Israel as is its usage in Acts 1:3 and 6. Hence we may note that when Jesus speaks of the Kingdom in the Gospels, it is in reference to offering the earthly Kingdom to Israel.

There are 7 references in Acts. Other than the first two found in Acts 1 all of the other references relate to the church in the sharing of the Gospel (Acts 28:23,31).

There are 18 additional references to the Kingdom recorded in the Epistles and five more in the Book of the Revelation almost all of which relate to the church. For example, I Corinthians 15:20-24: *"But now is Christ risen from the dead, and become the firstfruits of them that slept. For since by man came death, by man came also the resurrection of the dead. For as in Adam all die, even so in Christ shall all be made alive. But every man in his own order: Christ the firstfruits; afterward they that are Christ's at His coming. Then cometh the end, when he shall have delivered up the kingdom unto God, even the Father, when he shall have put down all rule and all authority and power."* Obviously, this is a reference to the church being caught up in the rapture. You may also want to read Colossians 1:13; James 2:5; and II Peter 1:10-11.

As we have already seen, the declaration is that Jesus is the Messiah, the Son of the Living God. Therefore, the faith the New Testament local church is to proclaim is salvation through the Messiah who is true God and that one can only enter into this new fellowship through faith in Jesus who is God. The design of this new fellowship is that it is to be an example on earth of the heavenly Kingdom. We will look at this issue in more detail later. A local church cannot be a spiritual maturing New Testament local church except it understand its purpose to be an example to the world of the heavenly kingdom that is to come, thus necessitating the practicing of the Kingdom principles.

THE DEMONSTRATION

Third, in this new society the righteousness of the kingdom is to be found. This is the message of the last part of Matthew 16:19: *"And whatsoever thou shalt bind on earth shall be bound in heaven: and whatsoever thou shalt loose on earth shall be loosed in heaven."* This indicates that in the meetings of the local church, not only are they to worship, but God's word is to be both taught and preached necessitating a pastor/ teacher. Discipleship is the major issue. The proclamation of God's Word through faithful men should be received as such: God's Word. But because I am still human and can err, when I was a pastor, I always encouraged my people to bring their Bibles and follow me. I told them often that, if they could not see what I was seeking to teach as valid in God's Word to "Always believe the Word." I learned early in my ministry not to be offended by those who might disagree with me. But to recognize these as opportunities to correct what needed to be corrected and be strengthened in those things in which I was already confident. I have believed for a long time that no teacher or preacher of the word should ever stand to teach or preach until he has absolute peace that what he is about to share is "Thus saith the Lord!"

This is the kind of preaching/teaching that will build the local church into a place where the righteousness of the Kingdom will be found. Is that not the essence of our Lord's command found in Matthew 6:33 where He said: *"Seek ye first the kingdom of God and His righteousness; and all these things shall be added unto you."*? A biblical local church, then, is to reflect and demonstrate in their life and practice the righteousness of the coming Kingdom.

This demands changed lives among the believers in both their life and actions. The local church is to be a family whose members love one another unconditionally (John 15:12,17). Paul describes the local fellowship as a body fitly put together that functions as a unit in harmony with each member working out his special gift(s) in unity with all the other members (I Cor. 12).

Paul also informed us that: *"We all, with open face beholding as in a glass the glory of the Lord, are changed into the same image from glory to glory even as by the Spirit of the Lord."* (II Cor. 3:18). This is a process that begins the moment we are saved and does not end until we are called home to be with Him. We, as believers, are called to holiness: *"I beseech you therefore, brethren, by the mercies of God, that you present your bodies a living sacrifice, holy, acceptable unto God, which is your reasonable service."* (Rom. 12:1). This is to be accomplished through *"the renewing of your mind."* (Rom. 12:2). This begins with the faithful teaching of God's word and precepts which should result in faithful obedience to that Word; which then results in a holy fellowship (John 14:23). The church body, then, is called to demonstrate on earth the righteousness of God's heavenly Kingdom and this can only become a reality in an organized local church where God's Word (all of it!) is faithfully proclaimed by faithful men and practiced by Godly members of the fellowship. Now there is a goal for every local church today to shoot for!

So we see the local church is constituted of believers in Messiah Jesus from every walk of life, both Jew and Gentile, (Ephesians 2:11-22) whose lives are being transformed by the teaching and preaching of God's Word.

This very first reference to the "church" (Matthew 16:18) is teaching that God, through the fellowship of the local church, is seeking to prepare the believer for eternity in the heavenly Kingdom which makes this our responsibility. It also indicates that the local church must be about the business of practicing what they preach creating a holy fellowship walking in obedience to God's Word. God's purpose for every local church is to establish a living example of life in the future Kingdom. Does this describe your church? Remember, these are just the fundamental truths! So whatever else the church is commanded to be and do will, in some way, directly connect with these three foundational truths. Therein is the key to understanding what a New Testament local Church should be.

Remember the three "D's: the Declaration; the Design; and the Demonstration. The true local church is constituted of believers in Jesus as the Messiah/ Redeemer, the very God, whose lives are being transformed thereby. This passage also teaches that God through the fellowship of the local church, is seeking to show to the world what God's eternal Kingdom will be like. It teaches that a true New Testament local church will be about the business of practicing what they preach, thus creating a holy fellowship walking in obedience to God's holy Word in accordance with the words of Jesus found in John 14:21-24.

Here are the three goals toward which every maturing New Testament local church should be striving. Whatever else a local church may be doing, it must connect, in some way, directly to these three fundamental truths laid out for us by our Lord in Matthew 16:13-19. Let us now move forward and look deeper into what the Bible teaches about what a local church should be.

e

CHAPTER 3

THE GREAT COMMISSION

We have already noted that God's purpose for the establishment of a local church on earth is to establish a working example of what life will be like in the heavenly Kingdom. This now raises the question of how that is to be accomplished. As we shall see, this is to be accomplished in two very specific activities. Let us now consider the first of those activities.

God's purpose in creating man was for the purpose of fellowship. As God is holy and only that which is holy can fellowship in holiness, man's sin (rebellion) thus hindered that fellowship which has always been God's desire for man. Peter wrote, as found in II Peter 3:9, that: *"the Lord is not slack concerning his promise, as some men count slackness; but is longsuffering to us-ward, not willing that any should perish, but that all should come to repentance."* One fundamental characteristic of a New Testament local church is their stand on the Scriptures as the verbal, plenary, inerrant, inspired word of God. A true New Testament local church believes that the Bible is to be understood and taken literally and so practiced. They should take seriously the words of Jesus found in John 14:23 where he states: *"If a man love me, he will keep my words: and my Father will love him, and we will come unto him. And make our abode with him."* Jesus also said: *"Ye are my friends, if ye do whatsoever I command you."* (John 15:14). So a true biblical New Testament local church will not pick and choose from God's Word what they will or will not do. They will seek to be obedient to it all.

The great challenge to the church today is the fulfillment of the Great Commission. We are not just asked, we are commanded to evangelize the world. The most often quoted passage used to define the Great Commission is Matthew 28:19-20. Dr. H. A. Ironside correctly stated that: "The Great Commission to evangelize the world is not given as a whole in any of the Gospels, but we need to take all related passages in the three synoptics and Acts 1 to get it in its entirety."i Though each has its unique emphasis, all state that the Gospel is to be proclaimed to all peoples of the world. Matthew declares that we are to *"Go ye therefore and teach all nations…"* (Matthew 28:19a).

Mark gives us the most basic statement: *"Go ye into all the world, and preach the Gospel to every creature"* (Mark 16:15"). Luke states: *"and that repentance and remission of sins should be preached in his name among all nations, beginning in Jerusalem."* (Luke 24:47). Luke, in Acts 1:8, puts the command to share the Gospel in the imperative: *"Ye shall"*. Therefore, understanding and carrying out the Great Commission is to be, for every believer (thus the local church), a priority (Matthew 6:33). All of the accounts agree that the message is to be carried to all people the world over. So it is clear that the Gospel is to be shared with both Jew and Gentile.

According to Matthew, the Great Commission includes both the sharing of the Gospel followed up with discipling them into the faith. Matthew emphasizes discipleship. Mark emphasizes evangelism. Luke emphasizes the content of the Gospel. Paul gives us the clearest statement of the content of the Gospel when he wrote: *"For I delivered unto you first of all that which I also received, how that Christ died for our sins according to the scriptures; and that he was buried, and that he arose again on the third day according to the scriptures."* (I Corinthians 15:3-4). This is the message we are commanded to carry to the world, to all people. So the first great challenge to the church is evangelize the world and disciple all new believers into the faith.

GOD'S PROGRAM FOR WORLD EVANGELISM

God's program for world evangelism includes two aspects: The reaching of the lost in our immediate area (our Jerusalem) and world missions (to the uttermost parts of the earth). Missions includes two parts: our own country and overseas. Many today often overlook the needs of our own county, state and country as a mission field. Yet, Acts 1:8 clearly states that we are commanded to take the gospel to "Jerusalem" (our community), Judea (our state), Samaria (our country) and also to the rest of the world (overseas).

God's Word gives us clear instruction as to His program for world evangelism and how it is to be carried out. First, He makes the message clear. It is a message of repentance and remission of sins (Luke 24:47). It is a message of God's love (John 3:16). It also is the message of the death, burial and resurrection of Israel's Messiah, the Lord Jesus, the true God, and its purpose that He died for our sins (I Corinthians 15: 4). This is the Good News that, if one believes and receives it, he is brought into a right relationship with his creator.

Second, God makes clear who is to deliver this message. Paul wrote in II Corinthians 5:18: *"And all things are of God, who hath reconciled us to himself by Jesus Christ, and hath given to us the ministry of reconciliation."* In verse 19 he restates it. In verse 20 he confirms our calling: *"Now then we are ambassadors for Christ."* And what does an ambassador do? He delivers the King's message, not his own. All believers are thus commanded to be the messenger of God's Good News to a lost and dying world (Acts 1:8).

Third, God clearly states in Romans 1:16 the method to be used. *"For I am not ashamed of the gospel of Christ: for it is the power of God unto salvation; to the Jew first and also to the Greek."* The key to understanding the latter part of this verse is found in defining the word: "first" (proton). William R. Newell states the generally accepted view. "In expressing *to the Jew first* Paul is not at all prescribing an order of presentation of the gospel throughout this dispensation. He is simply recognizing the fact that to the Jew, who had the law and divine privileges, the gospel offer had first been presented, and then to the Gentile."[ii] So he defines, as do most, the word "first" to simply mean historical sequence. The Greek word "proton" is often used in that sense (Matthew 5:24; 7:5; 13:30; Romans 15:24). However, it is also used by Jesus to denote <u>both</u> priority and sequence (Matthew 6: 33). As the Bible is of no private interpretation we must look to the contextual evidence to determine how it was used by Paul.

Paul also used the term in Romans 2:9-10. The use of the word "first" here cannot mean historical sequence. It simply states that both Jew and Gentile will be judged for bad or good. Charles Hodge, in his commentary on Romans wrote: "The Jew shall not only be punished as certainly others, but more severely, because he has been more highly favored. 'The Jew first' is equivalent then to the Jew especially."[iii] There will be a greater judgment upon the Jew (Leviticus 26:18-28). The Bible teaches that to whom much is given, much will be required (Luke 12:48). Much was given to the Jew. Paul wrote: *"What advantage hath the Jew? Or what profit is there of circumcision? Much every way: chiefly, because that to them was committed the oracles of God."* (Romans 3:1- 2) (Psalm 103:7; 147:19-20). Thus Paul uses the term "proton" to indicate both priority and sequence. Also, as one reads of Paul's travels, in every instance, though he viewed himself as the "Apostle to the Gentiles" (Romans 11:13) he went first to the Jews and then to the Gentiles he established an example and confirmed his understanding of God's plan for world evangelism. "To the Jew first" in Romans 1:16 teaches, as seen in Paul's consistent use of the term, both priority and sequence as is the only solution when you compare scripture with scripture.

One other word to consider in our text is the word "also" (kai). To understand "first" to indicate priority does not mean priority to the exclusion of the Greek (Gentile). "Also" shows that Gentiles are also included. Thus Paul states that, though we have a divinely stated special responsibility to carry the Gospel to the Jew (Romans 11:11, 30-31), we are also to take the Gospel to both Jew and Gentile, not eliminating either.

PAUL'S EXAMPLE

Though Paul recognized himself as "the Apostle to the Gentiles", in all of his recorded missionary journeys he always went first to the Jews. Paul's conversion is recorded in Acts chapter nine. In verse 15 we find the record of his call to take the Gospel to the Gentiles. Yet verse 20 reads: *"And straightway he preached Christ in the Synagogues."* Isn't it interesting that Paul began his ministry to the Gentiles by preaching first to the Jews? In Acts 13 the church at Antioch separated Paul and Barnabas *"for the work whereunto I have called them."* (verse 2). Now notice verse 5: *"And when they were in Salamis, they preached the word of God in the Synagogues of the Jews."* Then, in verse six, when they arrived in Paphos they *"found a certain sorcerer; a false prophet, a Jew, whose name was Bar-Jesus."* This man just happened to be a Jew which indicates that they sought out this particular man because he was Jewish. According to Acts 14:1, after leaving Antioch, they went to Iconium where *"they went both together into the Synagogue of the Jews, and so spake, that a great multitude both of the Jews and also of the Greeks believed."* Are you beginning to see a pattern? Again, in Acts 18:1-2 we see the same phrase used. *"After these things Paul departed from Athens, and came to Corinth; and found a certain Jew named Aquila."* Again, Paul searched out a Jewish person. Acts 18: 4 further states that while Paul remained in Corinth *"he reasoned in the Synagogue every Sabbath, and persuaded the Jews and the Greeks."*

Notice further Paul's actions when he arrived at Thessalonica as recorded in Acts 17: -2. *"Now when they had passed through Amphipolis and Apollonia, they came to Thessalonica, where was a Synagogue of the Jews: and Paul, as his manner was, went in unto them, and three Sabbath days reasoned with them out of the scriptures."* By now Paul's pattern was clearly established. Notice what Luke said: *"As his manner was."* Really? Well, let us read what Paul did when he arrived at Berea. *"And the brethren immediately sent away Paul and Silas by night unto Berea: who coming thither went into the Synagogue of the Jews."* (Acts 17:10). Paul's next stop was Athens. Acts 17:16-17 states: *"Now while Paul waited for them at Athens, his spirit stirred him, when he saw the city was full of idolatry. Therefore disputed he in the Synagogue with the Jews, and with the devout persons, and in the market daily with them that met with him."* Again, he goes to everyone, but starting with the Jews.

In Acts 19, after leaving Corinth, Paul went to Ephesus where he *"went into the Synagogue, and spake boldly for the space of three months."* (verse 8). In verse 10 we are told that he continued there for about two years preaching to both Jew and Gentile. Are you noticing a subtle change here? This change began on his third missionary journey. At every new place Paul always sought out the Jews first. But by now his ministry was remarkably expanding to include both Jew and Gentile. Note Acts 20:21: *"Testifying both to the Jews, and also to the Greeks, repentance toward God, and faith toward our Lord Jesus Christ."* In his early days it was always to the Jew first. Now, as he returned to those places where he had started ministries, Paul continues to share the Gospel with both Jew and Gentile clearly following the principle established in

Romans 1:16. Always he shared the Gospel with everyone, with both Jew and Gentile.

Paul speaks of this subtle change in his testimony to King Agrippa found in Acts 26:19-20. *"Whereupon, O king Agrippa, I was not disobedient unto the heavenly vision: but shewed first unto them of Damascus, and at Jerusalem, and throughout all the coasts of Judea, and then to Gentiles, that they should repent and turn to God, and do works meet for repentance."* Throughout his whole ministry Paul demonstrated that God's plan for missions was to the Jew first and also unto the Greek.

Today we must recognize a special responsibility to carry the Gospel to the Jews while also sharing it with the Gentiles. If we are to be faithful to God's plan for evangelizing the world and thus be a true biblical New Testament local church we must take the Gospel to "every creature", both Jew and Gentile. Jewish people are not uniquely difficult to reach but [they] do need to be reached uniquely because this is a cross cultural ministry. If you do not know how to approach a Jewish person we, at Jewish Awareness Ministries, Inc. are prepared to help you learn how you may effectively share the gospel with them. If, for whatever reason, we determine we will not take the Gospel to a particular person or group, regardless of race or creed, we are being disobedient to God's clear command. Thus we can no longer claim to be a Bible believing New Testament local church. If every church planting ministry and mission agency were following the example of Paul, who demonstrated God's plan for world evangelism, there never would have been a need for a ministry with a primary focus on reaching the Jew.

REFORMED/DISPENSATIONAL THEOLOGY AND MISSIONS

The problem that confronts us in the twenty-first century is that many, who interpret Romans 1: 16 in the sense that it is only stating an historical truth, see it as a reason not to take the Gospel to the Jew today. Reformed Theology teaches, because Israel nationally rejected the Messiah when He came, that God has turned His back on Israel (the Jewish people) and that the church today is the Israel of the Bible.

One need look no further than Romans 11:1 which states: *"Hath God cast away his people? God forbid…"* going on to give several reasons to prove his point in verses 2-10 to biblically demonstrate the falsehood of this teaching.

Some years ago, I was asked to speak at a Hebrew/Christian Fellowship in St. Petersburg, FL. My message title caught everyone's attention: "How to Destroy the Jew". My text was Jeremiah 31:35-37. God promises to turn His back on Israel if we can do one of two things: destroy the sun, moon and stars, or measure the universe. As neither can be done He goes on to state in the next verses that His relationship with Israel will last forever. After all, it is based on the unconditional Abrahamic Covenant.

Reformed theologians attempt to get around this by stating that today the church is Israel. They claim the New Covenant found in Jeremiah 31:31-34 was made with the church and not Israel. Yet in Jeremiah 31:31 God states: *"I will make a new covenant with the house of Israel and with the house of Judah."* These two "houses" denote the northern and southern kingdoms (physical Israel and Judah), not some spiritual entity. God is very specific as with whom He is making this covenant. Some dispensationalists make the same error by suggesting that, because we are living in the dispensation of the church, God has set the Jew aside. This is based upon a misunderstanding that Israel and Jew are synonymous. They are not. In this dispensation God is not dealing with the Jew nationally but individually, just as He is with Gentiles. (II Corinthians 3:12-16).

Some dispensationalists teach that all Jews will be saved at the time of Christ's second coming to establish the Kingdom. Yet the Bible teaches that only those who personally receive Christ as Saviour will be saved in any generation. All others will be eternally lost. Others teach that the Jews, even in this dispensation, are saved today by keeping the law. Jesus, speaking to the Jews debunked this when He said: *"I am the way the truth and the life; <u>no man cometh unto the father but by me</u>* (John 14: 6).

THE UNIQUE RELATIONSHIP OF THE JEW TO GOD

Another indicator of how Romans 1:16 is to be understood is found in the unique relationship the Jew has with God. In Deuteronomy 7: 6 it is recorded: *"For thou art an holy people unto the LORD thy God: the LORD Thy God hath chosen thee to be a special people unto himself, above all people that are upon the face of the earth."* This is restated in Deuteronomy 10: 14-15 and has never been rescinded by God. Isaiah describes this new relationship between God and the Jew. *"Can a woman forget her sucking child, that she should not have compassion on the son of her womb? Yea, they may forget, yet will I not forget thee. Behold I have graven thee upon the palms of my hands; thy walls are continually before me."* (Isaiah 49: 15-16). Neither covenants nor dispensations can negate this great truth. In light of this great truth, how can we, who claim to be saved and thus have God's heart, not love them as does God?

If you would like a definition of a true Biblical New Testament local Church in regard to how we are to keep the great Commission, you need look no further than Ephesians 2:13-18. *"But now in Christ Jesus ye who were sometimes far off* (Gentiles) *are made nigh by the blood of Christ. For he is our peace, who hath made both one* (Jew and Gentile), *and hath broken down the middle wall of partition between us; having abolished in his flesh the enmity, even the law of commandments contained in ordinances; for to make in himself of twain one new man, so making peace; and that he might <u>reconcile both unto God in one body by the cross, having slain the enmity thereby</u>: and came and preached peace to you which were afar off (Gentiles), and to them that were nigh (Jews). <u>For through him we both have access by one Spirit unto the Father</u>."*

CONCLUSION

The Great Commission is the command to carry the Gospel to both Jew and Gentile, that is, to everyone. How else can the local church be made up of both Jew and Gentile except we recognize that the Jew is included in the great Commission and except we be obedient to His command?

Romans 1:16 unambiguously states God's program for world evangelization. Paul's missionary journeys clearly establish the sense of priority to the Jew, while yet taking the Gospel to the Gentiles. Perhaps God knew that some in the church would refuse, for whatever their reason, to take the Gospel to the Jew, so He has given us no wiggle room by emphasizing that we are to take the gospel even to the Jew.

The true local church should reflect in its membership the people groups living in their outreach area, if they are being faithful to the Great Commission. Does the membership of your fellowship reflect the people groups that make up the neighborhoods surrounding your church? This is a clear indicator of the degree of your obedience to the Great Commission

The reasons given by those for not evangelizing the Jew do not stand the test of sound biblical exegesis. No matter the time frame, we are responsible to take the Gospel to both Jew and Gentile, in other words to everyone. God's unique relationship with Israel and the Jew demands that Romans 1:16 be understood to be speaking of priority. God said to Abraham regarding his seed: *"I will bless them that bless thee and curse him that curseth thee."* To share the Gospel with the Jew is to receive a blessing. How can we better bless the Jew than to share with him the Gospel or curse him than by withholding from them the Gospel (I Corinthians 10:32).

I wonder how many otherwise sound biblical ministries, both mission agencies and local churches already established, are following God's clearly stated and biblically demonstrated plan for world evangelization? What can we do to be in obedience to the Lord in His clear plan to evangelize His world? Whether it be an individual, a local church, or a mission agency, there are at least four things we can do to be in conformity with God's plan for world evangelization:

1.   Include the Jew in your outreach ministries. If you are a church planter, follow Paul's example and God will bless you.

2.   Recognize that, if you have Jewish families in your outreach area, it is your responsibility before God to evangelize them.

3.   As Jewish evangelism is a cross cultural ministry as is reaching Muslims and other ethnic groups, invite an informed missionary working with Jewish people to instruct you as to how you can have the opportunity to effectively share the Gospel with Jewish folks.

4.   Pray regularly for the peace of Jerusalem (Psalm 122: 6), for in so doing, you are praying for their salvation and God will bless you and your ministry.

As the Great Commission is a clear command to every believer, and thus to the local church, to evangelize all people a local church cannot qualify as a biblical New Testament local church if they are refusing, for whatever their reason, to reach out with the Gospel to ALL people.

e

CHAPTER 4

DISCIPLESHIP

As we come to the subject of discipleship, in the first place, we need to understand that the Christian life involves two things: birth and growth. When a woman delivers a baby into this world does she get up from the delivery table and say: "Well, I have done my job," and then goes home without taking the baby home with her? Of course not! Why? Is it not because the greatest part of birthing a child into this world is taking it home and discipling it into the human race? And yet, so often, soul winners will birth someone into the Kingdom, but do nothing to disciple him/her into the faith.

Years ago, when we started Fellowship Bible Baptist Church in the inner city of Baltimore, Maryland, I quickly learned that I had four to six months to disciple our new believers into the faith before they moved out of the inner city and went back home. As most were at least second or third generation welfare people, they had little self-respect. But when they were saved and discovered that God loved them, all that changed and they realized they did not have to live that way anymore. So every Tuesday evening, for one hour I taught them the doctrines of the Biblical faith. Today, even after fifty years, we still occasionally run into someone that we had led to the Lord and discipled in the faith from those days who were still going on in their walk with the Lord. That is a blessing!

While living in St. Petersburg, FL back in the 1980s we were familiar with a fundamental church that had a strong evangelism program and bus ministry. They had teams out on the streets almost six days a week. As decisions were made they brought them back to the church and baptized them. The problem was that the church (when we first knew it,) was running over 200 in attendance in their services. Every year they were announcing over 900 decisions for Christ, but the church continued to diminish until they were down to less than

100. What was going on? One of their deacons attended regularly our Hebrew/ Christian Bible study. He told me about going to the pastor and asking why they did not have a discipleship ministry for new believers. He told me that the pastor's response was: "Our responsibility is to get them saved. It is the Holy Spirit's responsibility to disciple them." And yet, the Bible states in Matthew 28:20 that we are to teach them (new believers) *"to observe whatsoever I have commanded you…"* That is a command to disciple them into the faith.

We are commanded to teach new babes in Christ the Biblical faith. Notice God's plan for all new believers. Paul stated it in II Corinthians 3:18. *"But we all, with open face beholding as in a glass the glory of the Lord, are changed into the same image from glory to glory."* "Glory to glory" indicates a process. And how does this happen? Paul states in II Timothy 3:16: *"All scripture is given by inspiration of God, and is profitable for doctrine, for reproof, for correction, for instruction in righteousness: that the man of God may be perfect, thoroughly furnished unto all good works."* Again, in Romans 15:4 Paul wrote: *"For whatsoever things are written aforetime were written for our learning, that we through patience and comfort of the scriptures might have hope."* Discipleship is accomplished through the systematic teaching of God's Word. Salvation occurs when one by faith receives Christ as Saviour. In Romans 10:17 Paul wrote *"So then faith cometh by hearing, and hearing by the word of God."* It is the hearing of God's word that stimulates saving faith.

The believer is admonished to live by faith. But how? Peter, in II Peter 1:2-4 clearly states how this is to be accomplished. *"Grace and peace be multiplied unto you through the knowledge of God, and of Jesus our Lord, according as the divine power hath given unto us all things that pertain unto life and godliness, through the knowledge of him that hath called us to glory and virtue: whereby are given unto us exceeding great and precious promises: that by these ye might be partakers of the divine nature, having escaped the corruption that is in the world through lust."*

Discipleship is to be done precept upon precept and line upon line. For more information on how to effectively accomplish this you will find "Twelve Steps to Spiritual Maturity" in my book entitled *"WORSHIP, AN AWESOME JOURNEY OF FAITH"* which is available by contacting me.

26

Discipleship needs more than just preaching three times a week. It takes personal or class instruction in the basic truths of the faith in such a manner that the new believer can understand not only the truth we are seeking to teach them but its relationship to the previous and following truths. A concentrated discipleship program for a new believer establishes the foundation for their further growth in their walk with the Lord. It will prepare them to respond positively to the teaching/preaching of the Word in our regular services

The focus needs to be primarily on three fundamental issues: Jesus, righteousness and the Word of God. Because our culture today teaches that if your good works outweigh your bad works you are a good person, the first issue with which we should deal is that it only takes one sin to be a sinner. Adam is the primary example of this great truth, and it helps them to more fully understand why one needs to be saved. This truth needs to be connected to the Doctrine of God, specifically an understanding of His holiness. In understanding who Jesus is, they need to understand the Old Testament teachings about the Messiah. Not only will this help them to better understand who He is and His work accomplished on Calvary, but will help them to also understand that our Bible is truly one book.

Righteousness is a primary goal in the Christian walk (Matthew 6:33; Galatians 5:18-26) as the goal is to transform the new believer into the very image of Christ (II Corinthians 3:18). Any study that seeks to teach righteousness must be founded in the teaching of the very character of the triune God. Remember, the local New Testament Church is to be an example of the future Kingdom.

New believers need to be taught how to read their Bible with understanding. In my book entitled *"Understanding God's Program for the Ages"*, which is a study of Biblical Covenants and dispensations, will help a new believer to understand the flow and development of Biblical truths. This information is essential if one is to rightly divide the word of truth. If you need further help in putting such a program together there are many other helpful books on the shelf in any good Bible Book Store.

When I was still functioning as a pastor, I did one other thing in relation to the discipleship process. I taught my soul winners to teach their new believers the very fundamental truths necessary to get them growing in their new-found faith. The soul winner should be responsible to get them started attending the worship services. They need also to see that they have a Bible and help them get started reading it. One good way to do that is for the soul winner to meet with them for a few weeks to help them study and understand the Gospel of John or some other good starting point. Then we should move them into what I chose to call an advanced discipleship class that includes, among other things, how they could be effective soul winners in order to reproduce themselves.

I consistently taught our people soul winning. And they all had to complete the advanced discipleship class. A solid discipleship program is absolutely necessary if your church is to qualify as a Biblical New Testament local church. Remember, a true biblical local church will be "Saviour" sensitive and not "seeker" sensitive. A "seeker" sensitive ministry leads the church to compromise with the world in order not to offend the "seeker".

DISCIPLESHIP AND THE LOCAL CHURCH AS A BODY

Paul stated in I Corinthian 12:12: *"For as the body is one, and hath many members, and all the members of that one body, being many, are one body: so also is Christ."* Regarding this body, Paul further taught that *"There are diversities of gifts, but the same Spirit."* He goes on to show how diverse the gifts are in verses 4- 11.

To every believer in every local fellowship there is given at least one spiritual gift. Is it not true, that among his other responsibilities, it is the pastor's work to help his people discern their spiritual gifts? Then, in relation to the gift, find the place within the fellowship where each member best fits in serving the Lord. Has not God found the proper place for each diverse part of the physical body that allows it to function properly and productively? Yet, is this not an issue that is generally overlooked, that if made a priority in the church, would cause the church to function more efficiently and productively? If we are to take this passage literally, it teaches us that there is a working place for every member that will cause the church to become a well-oiled and functioning body of believers. This function is best accomplished hand in hand with the teaching side of the discipleship issue.

CONCLUSIONS

Discipleship is related to the New Birth which is a new beginning. (II Corinthians 3:17-18; Romans 8:29). God's purpose is to create a fellowship of believers that exemplifies to the world what God's heavenly kingdom will be like. (Matthew 6:33; Luke 12:31).

Discipleship must teach true biblical principles to enable the new believer to make godly choices and righteous decisions. They need to understand what the Bible teaches is the true motivation that leads to godly living, unconditional (Divine) love. (John 14:15,21,23; 15:12).

Discipleship is necessary to teach an understanding of the faith which is comprised of biblical doctrines and practice. It should also teach that God has a plan for each life (Psalm 16:11), how to find it, and why it is better than any other plan. They need to understand that this plan includes the use of their spiritual gifts as a part of a true healthy Bible- believing local church.

Discipleship is necessary to help the new believer understand the value of being an integral part of a true Bible believing local church that practices what it teaches. Only with this information will the new believer be able to make right decisions in implementing the changes the Holy Spirit is seeking to bring about in the transformation of their life.

Without a solid and biblically sound discipleship plan a local church cannot qualify as a truly biblical New Testament local Church. Without it the fellowship will not develop as God intends. Evangelism without discipleship produces only carnal Christians. Does your church have a sound and effective discipleship program? If not, it cannot qualify as a biblical New Testament local Church.

e
CHAPTER 5

THE CHURCH'S MINISTRY TO ONE ANOTHER

The local church is absolutely essential for the growth of the believer. We need to recognize that every member of the fellowship is an important part of that growth process, not just the pastor, deacons and Sunday School teachers. This is an area of our church ministry that is so often overlooked that is really important to understand. Without it the church is not functioning biblically and thus cannot be considered a New Testament local church. In this chapter we shall explore the believer's ministry to one another in the church fellowship.

THE MOTIVATION

First, we must note the motivation behind a right relationship among believers. In John 14:21 Jesus states: *"He that hath my commandments, and keepeth them, he it is that loveth me: and he that loveth me shall be loved by my Father, and I will love him, and will manifest myself to him."* In John 15:12 Jesus states: *"This is my commandment, that ye love one another, as I have loved you."* In John 13:34-35 we read again the words of Jesus saying: *"A new commandment I give unto you, that ye love one another; as I have loved you, that ye also love one another."* Paul reinforces our Lord's commandment in Ephesians 5:2; 1 Thessalonians 5:9; I Peter 1:22.

Understand the love of which He speaks. In the Greek it is *agape* which is "unconditional" love. It is a sacrificial love. In John 15:13 He defines this love: *Greater love hath no man than this, that a man lay down his life for his friends."* Note the words of John recorded in I John

3:16. *"Hereby perceive we the love of God, because He laid down His life for us; and we aught to lay down our lives for the brethren."*

Occasionally I have the opportunity to preach on this issue. I will usually ask: *"Look around the room. Is there anyone here that, if the circumstances warranted, you would be unwilling to die for that person? If you answer, yes, then are you not out of fellowship with our Lord?"* The basic motive for all that we do is to be a divine unconditional love working in our heart and life, just like Jesus.

Paul makes the practical application for us in Romans 13:10 where he wrote: *"Love worketh no ill to his neighbor: therefore love is the fulfilling of the law."* cf. Matthew 22:37-40. Here the application is broadened for the law said: *"Thou shalt love thy neighbor as thyself."* (Leviticus 19:18). So we see that love, not righteousness, is the fundamental active principle of the Christian faith. And that love is to be demonstrated both to the church family and to all people.

The important lesson here is that only those empowered by the Holy Spirit can so love. Only the believer has been given a new life that enables him to love as God loves. It is this distinction that sets the Christian apart from the rest of the world and is to be practiced in the fellowship. Remember, the local church is to be an example of life in the heavenly Kingdom.

THE OUTWORKING OF THE LOVE PRINCIPLE

Consider Hebrews 10:23-25. *"Let us hold fast the profession of our faith without wavering; (for he is faithful that promised;) and let us consider one another to provoke unto love and good works: Not forsaking the assembling of ourselves together, as the manner of some is; but exhorting one another: and so much the more, as ye see the day approaching."*

In verses 19 to 22 Paul states the faith to which we are to hold fast. *"Having therefore, brethren, boldness to enter into the holiest by the blood of Jesus, by a new and living way, which he hath consecrated for us, through the veil, that is to say, his flesh; and having an high priest over the house of God; let us draw near with a true heart in full assurance of faith, having our hearts sprinkled from an evil conscience, and our bodies washed with pure water."* Herein the author describes the faith that gives direct access to the very throne of God. This faith is based solely upon the shed blood of God's Son, Israel's Messiah, the Lord Jesus. We are admonished to hold this faith in total commitment because He is our faithful high priest. *"Seeing then that we have a great high priest, that is past into the heavens, Jesus the Son of God, let us hold fast our profession."* (Hebrews 4:14).

"But the Lord is faithful, who shall stablish you, and keep you from evil." (II Thessalonians 3:3). We are encouraged not to allow anything to shake our faith in God as was the example of Job. We are called to believe what we have professed and be what we claim to be. We are to let our faith work out in our life as a clear testimony to all the world of the reality of our Saviour and our God.

It is this very visible faith that becomes the basis for our relationship with other believers. Herein we see the importance of being a part of a godly local fellowship. As the world is constantly attacking us, just assembling together to worship is an act of encouraging one another to stay faithful. This is to be more than a passive act. It is to be an ongoing opportunity to gain strength from one another. But it is also the opportunity to come beside a brother or sister who is wavering as we share words of encouragement and buy up the opportunity to share the Word of God to strengthen them in their growing process. In this way we may stimulate them to greater love and good works. This is an opportunity to help one another find their spiritual gift(s) and thereby find where they fit within the fellowship itself. These are all opportunities to comfort, strengthen and build up one another in the faith. This is how it will be in the heavenly Kingdom. So now we are actually demonstrating, both to one another and to the world, what that Kingdom will be like when we get there. Is that not, as we have seen, God's clear intention for the local church?

CONCLUSION

Participation in a true Bible believing/practicing local church is absolutely essential for a believer to be obedient to God's plan and personal growth in the faith. One of the immediate steps in the discipleship process is involving the new believer in the local church. The problem is that we often view salvation as an end in itself rather than a new beginning, a new birth. If they really are saved, they should immediately have a hunger for spiritual food as a baby has a built-in hunger for physical food.

In our first street meeting on a Friday night in Baltimore, Randy, who was fifteen at the time and a typical hippy, was hanging out his second story window observing the meeting right under his window. When the invitation was given he came down and, with the help of one of our counselors, received Christ as his Saviour. He knew that this meeting was being held by Fellowship Bible Baptist Church which was just a block away. We did announce our services and extended an invitation to any who might be interested. Sunday morning Randy showed up wearing his best suit and had a real haircut. Randy grew spiritually. He played the guitar and began to sing Gospel music. We quickly involved him in our street ministry team where he became a real blessing and a gift to our ministry. He came to church that Sunday because he was both hungry and curious. We did not have to twist his arm because he truly got saved that Friday night! Oh, that that would happen with everyone who makes a profession of faith!

The local church is the place where believers can and should grow together with their spiritual family and parents, who are the Word and the Holy Spirit. (John 3:5). Is this what is happening in your church? This is what the Lord has intended the church to be.

There are many other issues that are at work in a good local church. But everything should connect in some way to the three foundational truths: The DECLARATION, the DESIGN, and the DEMONSTRATION.

Sunday School should be a major source of systematically grounding the students in the fundamental truths of the faith, regardless of the age group being taught. Soul winning should be consistently taught to the teens and adults along with regular opportunities to put these teachings into practice for both groups.

The music ministry of the church should be Christ honoring, both in the words and in the music and how it is presented. I lead the congregational music at our church. I try to theme the hymns in order to build a meaningful worship experience. As a matter of habit I generally screen all special music.

No matter the issue in what is being done, it should fit in one of the three biblical fundamental purposes for a biblical New Testament local church laid out in the early chapters of this book. In worship what we do should always help the worshippers to focus on Christ and the Word. Again, my earlier book entitled "Worship, An Awesome Journey of Faith"

where I developed twelve principles of worship should be a real help to you in understanding worship and how to consistently make public worship a blessed experience.

e

CHAPTER 6

EPILOGUE

Our question has been: "How do we identify a biblical New Testament local church?" The answer is quite simple, though it has several parts.

First, it is important for us to understand at the very outset that the local church is not brick and mortar, but flesh and blood. The true church is made up of true believers in Christ who have come together both to worship and to serve our living Lord.

Second, it is important that we understand God's goal for establishing a local church. We have learned that there are 154 "Kingdom" references in the New Testament, most of which are clearly referencing the local church. God's primary intent for establishing a local church is that it is to be representative of the heavenly Kingdom realized on earth. All through the New Testament the message is that, when one receives Christ as Saviour, one's life is to change. This makes one uniquely different from the rest of the world and is emphatic. Every local church should illustrate in its life and activities what the coming eternal Kingdom is going to be like. As this is God's clear intent for the local church, if your church is not consciously seeking to so demonstrate in its life and activities, it cannot qualify as a biblical New Testament local church.

Third, the Bible emphatically teaches that we are His ambassadors. An ambassador carries to the world the Lord's message. That message is His message of Redemption to be shared with every lost person which is made clear by the great Commission as discussed in chapter three of this book. It is the message of the New Birth. Unless a church is faithfully disseminating that evangelistic message to the lost world to all people, it cannot be a biblical New Testament local church.

Fourth, we are born as new babes into a new life. A major part of the ministry of a true biblical local church is to disciple these new babes into this new life. When one is truly born again he is filled with the Holy Spirit who empowers us to grow to maturity in the understanding and practice of this new life. This is the essence of Matthew 28:19-20. When one is born physically he is born hungry. So it is in the spiritual birth. Their hunger is only satisfied by the systematic teaching of God's Word. The goal of discipleship is beautifully stated by Paul in II Corinthians 3:18: *"But we all, with open face beholding as in a glass the glory of the Lord, are changed into the same image from glory to glory, even as by the Spirit of the Lord."* How we are called to accomplish this is shared in Chapter four of this book. Any local church that is not involved in a clear systematic discipleship ministry that seeks to involve new believers in the life and ministry of the church, cannot be a true New Testament local church.

Fifth, every believer is given at least one spiritual gift that needs to be identified and cultivated toward the end of using that gift in participating as a healthy part of the church family. This needs to be seen as a part of the discipleship process as it is an integral part of the spiritual growth process.

Sixth, as believers, why we do what we do and why we refrain from doing other things is the one issue that separates the true believer from the rest of the world. Jesus said: *"If a man love me, he will keep my words: and my Father will love him, and we will come unto him, and make our abode with him."* (John14:23). Years ago, a man who lived in West Virginia, and was the town drunk got saved. A few weeks after he was saved he stood up in his local church to share a testimony. He said: *"I give glory to Jesus because he changed my druthers."* He truly loved the Lord because he now knew that the Lord loved him.

What motivates us makes all the difference. We love Him because He first loved us. Then he calls us to love one another. As recorded in John 15:11 Jesus said: *"This is my commandment, that ye love one another, as I have loved you."* The word love here, in the Greek is "agape". This is unconditional love.

There is a day when every believer will stand before the Lord to be judged for what he did with his life from the day he was saved to the day that he wenthome to be with the Lord. Please read I Corinthians 3:9-15. Note in verse 14 that our works will be judged on the basis of what *"sort"* they are. He is talking motive. We can do the right thing for the wrong reason and lose our reward. The Greek word is *"hopios"* which denotes quality or motive. Jesus makes

clear, as we just quoted him, that the motive by which we will be judged is unconditional love. This is the quality of life that transforms one's life and separates a true Bible believing New Testament local church from all the rest. It is an empowerment of the indwelling Holy Spirit.

CONCLUDING THOUGHT

In conclusion, having shared all of these biblical thoughts as to what constitutes a biblical New Testament Church, we need to understand that there is no church that perfectly demonstrates all of these qualities. That is simply because right now we are still living in and are somewhat influenced by the flesh.

This will not be the case in the Heavenly Kingdom. But there are a few local fellowships around that are working to demonstrate all of the principles laid out in this book because they are faithfully seeking to please the Lord.

Remember, all of this can begin with just one person in a local fellowship who is willing to be used of the Lord to influence the changes necessary to bring that fellowship into conformity to God's plan for the local church. Do you love Him enough to be that person in your fellowship? The Holy Spirit who indwells you is the great enabler. Herein is the foundation for revival in your church. May the Lord enable you to be the instrument that God can use to bring this about in your church!

e
End Notes

i.   H.A. Ironside, Expository Notes on the Gospel of Matthew; 1948, Loizeaux Brothers; New York; p. 402

ii.   William R. Newel, Romans Verse by Verse; 1938, Moody Press; Chicago; p. 22

iii.   Charles Hodge, Commentary on the Epistle to the Romans; 1964, Wm. B. Erdmans Publishing Co.; Grand Rapids; p. 52

e
Bibliography

Alexander, Joseph A. *Commentary on the Acts of the Apostles*. Grand Rapids, MI: Zondervan Publishing House, 1956

Bruce, F. F. *Commentary on the Book of Acts*. Grand Rapids, MI: Wm B. Eerdmans Publishing Company, 1964

Greene, Oliver B. *The Epistle of Paul the Apostle to the Hebrews*. Greenville, SC: The Gospel Hour, 1965

Hodge, Charles. *Commentary on the Epistle to the Romans*. Grand Rapids, MI: Wm B. Eerdmans Publishing Co, 1964

Ironside, H. A. *Expository Notes on the Gospel of Matthew*. New York, NY: Loizeaux Brothers, Inc, 1948 Newell, William R. *Romans verse by Verse*. Chicago, IL.. Moody Press, 1938

Pink, Arthur W. *An exposition of Hebrews*. Grand Rapids, MI. Baker Book House, 1954

Walvoord, John F. *Matthew Thy Kingdom Come*. Chicago, IL. Moody Press, 1974

www.ingramcontent.com/pod-product-compliance
Lightning Source LLC
Chambersburg PA
CBHW051249120626
46547CB00014B/1865